31 Prayers for my future Wife

PREPARING MY HEART FOR MARRIAGE BY PRAYING FOR HER

AARON & JENNIFER SMITH

31 Prayers For My Future Wife

Preparing My Heart For Marriage By Praying For Her

Written By Aaron & Jennifer Smith
Edited By Cambria Jacobson & Stacy Mehan
Cover & Interior Design By Jane Johnson
Interior Format & Layout By Aaron Smith

Copyright © 2019 Smith Family Resources, Inc.

ISBN-10: 0-9863667-6-5
ISBN-13: 978-0-9863667-6-5
LCCN: 2016915323

31prayersformyfuturewife.com

Printed in U.S.A

Contents

God Hears Us

1 John 5:13−15

"I write these things to you who believe in the name of the Son of God, that you may know that you have eternal life. And this is the confidence that we have toward Him, that if we ask anything according to His will He hears us. And if we know that He hears us in whatever we ask, we know that we have the requests that we have asked of Him."

Introduction

Marriage is an incredible relationship that unifies two individuals, binding them together through their commitment to love each other, making them one. There is no other relationship on earth that can compare to the intimacy experienced in marriage as God designed it. Just like we become one with Jesus when we accept Him into our hearts, married together through a powerful covenant which He sacrificed Himself to provide, marriage is a reflection of this miraculous oneness. When a husband and wife love each other, they reflect that same love that motivated Christ. They die to themselves and become one.

I had a strong desire to get married young. As much as I wanted to get married and have someone to share my life with, I also had a selfish ambition to get married so that I could experience sexual intimacy. I was abstaining from sex because I wanted to remain pure for my wife, but the struggle was real. I craved sex. Although I wanted to get married and experience sexual satisfaction, I submitted my desires to God and waited for Him to present to me, my future wife.

In fact, I went through a season of not even dating. I had friends who I developed close relationships with, but I resisted dating to help me avoid the temptation of sex. I decided the next woman I dated would be someone I knew I would spend the rest of my life with. I dedicated time to getting closer to God, and I took time to write out specific prayers for my future wife.

I believed and trusted that God would provide for me a good wife. It was my commitment to prayer that helped me protect and prepare my heart for marriage. I looked forward to the day I would marry my best friend.

I had been pursuing a strong friendship with Jennifer when I felt God clearly reveal to me that she would be my wife one day. We moved forward in our relationship more seriously when I asked her to be my girlfriend. It was an amazing feeling to be able to turn my prayers for my future wife into more personal ones when I began praying for Jennifer and our future marriage.

When I got the courage to propose marriage to her I opened up my Bible and gave her a short stack of worn papers that had my handwriting all over them. As she read through each one I explained to her that I have had a strong desire to get married and have been praying for my future wife even before I had met her. Then I told her that she was my answer to prayer! She said yes to marriage, and the first thing we did that night as an engaged couple was pray for our future marriage. That moment was extremely memorable.

Getting married and knowing that God brought my wife and I together has been one of the best feelings in the world. There have been difficult times that have threatened our unity and almost destroyed our marriage, but the Lord has been faithful to answer both of our prayers for each other and for our marriage. Prayer has been the most powerful tool in saving and strengthening our marriage!

My wife and I can personally testify to the power of prayer, which is why we encourage others to have a heart dedicated to prayer. Through our online ministries (Husband Revolution & Unveiled Wife) we kept hearing one couple after another admit how difficult prayer is, how uncomfortable it is to pray for each other, and we have heard that some people just don't know how to pray. Hearing these stories moved us to write Thirty-One Prayers For My Wife and Thirty-One Prayers For My Husband. The feedback we receive from couples taking our 31 Prayer Challenge has been astounding. Testimonies continue to flood in from husbands and wives about how God is moving in their hearts and marriages.

We have been praising God for the breakthroughs marriages are experiencing because of these resources. However, there was this thought in the back of our minds about encouraging people to become prayer warriors before the wedding! We thought about the next generation of husbands and wives that need to know how to pray for each other and their relationship. We hope 31 Prayers For My Future Wife and 31 Prayers For My Future Husband inspire people's hearts to commit to praying for the marriage they hope to one day have, or the marriage they are in the process of planning for right now. Our hearts desire is to see men and women prepare their hearts for marriage by praying and petitioning to God for the hearts of their future spouse. We hope and pray that people who have a desire to have a God-centered marriage will take this prayer challenge to equip them for their future marriage.

We wrote this book because we want to help you and motivate you to pray for the wife you long for. We want you to be open and willing to pray for your future marriage. Most of all we want you to draw closer to God through the power of prayer! We also desire that when you do become a husband, you will have such a passionate and established prayer life, that the enemy can't knock you down.

This resource is not a magical book that will produce your future wife. Reading this book and praying these prayers will not guarantee that you will one day get married. However, the Bible is clear that we are to come to God and pray for everything.

"Do not be anxious about anything, but in everything by prayer and supplication with thanksgiving let your requests be made known to God." - Philippians 4:6 ESV

Praying for a future marriage that you hope for, will remind your heart not to worry, but rather trust in God and in His timing. Praying for your future wife is a request that God asks you to make known to Him. By faithfully praying for your future wife and future marriage, you are sharing your heart with God and letting him get to know you! Growing close to God, trusting Him with your heart, knowing Him, and being known by Him is true intimacy, and the very thing that will satisfy you!

As you submit your heart to God in prayer, you will see Him move! And how amazing it will be to one day hear a testimony from your future wife about how your prayers helped her! You can read these prayers straight from the text, you can say them out loud, you can get on your knees, or stand with your hands raised up toward the sky. There are also journal lines provided to make these prayers personal to you. You are God's son and He is going to be blessed hearing from you!

**I have included a few challenges to encourage you to consider the significance and purpose of prayer. There is a total of 7 challenges. I urge you to pray about each one and then fulfill it as the Lord leads you.*

****I also want to see your journey along the way! Update your social media and tag @husbandrevolution and #HR31Prayers so I can follow along and see how God is moving in your life!*

Dear Heavenly Father,

I pray over this book and ask that You would use it to inspire and encourage the reader to boldly enter into Your throne room on the behalf of his future bride. Give this man a heart after Your heart, and transform his character to reflect the character of Jesus. I pray You would show this man what a true spiritual leader looks like, and how You want to prepare him for his future bride. Lord, use this book as a launching pad for his spiritual journey to becoming a husband. Teach this man how to be a prayer warrior for not only his future wife, but also for his future children, his friends, and his community. Give him peace as he waits for the wife You are going to bring him, and give him patience to wait for Your timing and Your perfect will. Protect his heart and help him to pursue purity. May Your will be done in his life. May he surrender to You and trust You with all his heart, mind, soul, and strength. Transform this man and prepare him to be a leader and warrior for Your Kingdom.

In Jesus' name AMEN!

Her Heart

Mark 12:30

Dear Lord,

Thank You for my future wife. I pray You would bless her life. No matter where she is or what she is doing, I pray You would overwhelm her with Your love. Remind her every single day of her value and why You love her so much. I pray for her heart. I pray she surrenders her life to You, and that she passionately pursues a deeply intimate relationship with You. May she have the courage to let You get to know every part of her heart. If there is anything in her past that is causing her pain, please heal her completely. I pray she would learn to trust You for everything. I also pray she would learn to be completely satisfied by You. Send people into her life that will mentor her and encourage her. May these influencers guide her according to Your ways. I pray my future wife would love You with all of her heart, with all of her soul, with all of her mind, and with all of her strength. May Your Holy Spirit walk with her daily and teach her how to walk in all Your ways. Infuse her with confidence that will help her remain strong amidst a culture that is constantly pressuring women with worldly standards. Give her courage and boldness to live a life of righteousness and purity. Prepare her heart for marriage, and prepare her heart for me.

In Jesus' name AMEN!

Personalize

Use this area to write a personalized prayer for your future wife. You can also write a list of things you would like to continue to pray for.

Challenge
- #1 -

START A

prayer journal

Use this journal to write down your prayers,
especially your prayers for your future wife.

Begin your prayer journal by writing out
a personal prayer for your future wife.

Her Family

Exodus 20:12

Dear God,

I lift up my future wife to You today. Thank You for the gift of family. I pray for her relationship with her family. May Your Holy Spirit guide her in all of her relationships with immediate and extended family. Help her to set clear boundaries with them, while still respecting them. Use her to be a blessing to her family. Use her to be a light in their lives. I pray she honors You by honoring her parents. I pray she is respectful toward them and is an ambassador of Your truth to them. I pray she is an obedient daughter, but that she never forsakes Your statutes just to appease her family. I pray she responds to them with kindness leading her heart. I pray that if there are any relationships with family that cause pain, please bring reconciliation. I especially pray that my future wife has a strong relationship with her father. If there is any brokenness in their relationship, I pray You would help them both be mended. Help her to feel loved and cherished by him. I also pray she feels loved and cherished by You. I pray You would prepare her family for when she gets married. I pray You would prepare her family to accept me. I pray against any family feuds and any conflict that would try and persuade us to not get married. I pray Your will is done in our future relationship and that both of our families would support us and be unified through us.

In Jesus' name AMEN!

Personalize

Use this area to write a personalized prayer for your future wife. You can also write a list of things you would like to continue to pray for.

Her Worthiness

Psalm 139:13–15

Dear Heavenly Father,

Thank You for every detail You thought of when You formed my future wife. Thank You for the talents You gave her, and thank You for her purpose. I pray she knows how cherished she is by You. I pray her eyes are open to all the ways You love her. Holy Spirit, please reveal to her all the ways she is an image bearer of You. May she recognize all of the ways You are using her life to help others discover who You are. Help her to know that she is a reflection of You and Your amazing love. I pray she would let You know her intimately, sharing the depths of her heart with You. I pray she comes to fully know You. May Your relationship with her continue to mature and strengthen every single day. I pray her time with You is a priority and that she commits herself to prayer every day. Draw her close to You, Lord. Help her to know that You were intentional in the way You created her. I pray she sees her beauty, accepts herself, and is a confident woman. May she disregard the standard of beauty the world pressures women to measure up to, and instead trusts You and how You created her. Heal her of the pain she feels from the impact of negative words said to her. Reaffirm her through Your Word. Help her to embrace Your view of her, Your opinion of who she is! Help her to understand her worthiness.

In Jesus' name AMEN!

Her True Beauty

Proverbs 5:15-19

Dear Lord,

I pray my future wife will know that she is a reflection of Your image, and that she has been given a beautiful form that is delightful to my eyes and heart. I pray I would always be intoxicated by her love and beauty. You have said in Your Word that he who finds a wife, finds a good thing. Thank You for my good gift, and thank You for her beauty. Help her to believe that she truly is beautiful. I also pray she would not rely on validation from others to believe she is beautiful. May she seek approval from You only. May she have a positive self-image, and may she understand how her character and her love for You is a part of her true beauty. I pray she realizes her adoration for You is a huge part of her attractiveness. When she feels ugly, I pray You would use people in her life to show her the truth of her beauty. When she feels unattractive please use me to affirm her and overwhelm her with love and acceptance. I pray against shame and guilt from burdening her heart and tainting her perspective of herself. I pray against lies of the enemy that threaten to tear her down in any way. Lord, I pray my future wife walks in the truth that she is radiant because of Your light shining through her. I pray she would embrace the beauty You see in her. The beauty that comes from a heart submitted to You, and when we get married, a heart submitted to me. The beauty of a quiet and humble heart. The beauty of a gentle and kind spirit. Bless my future wife.

In Jesus' name AMEN!

Challenge

- #2 -

TAKE SOME
time to think

Consider all the ways God shows you His love.

Praise Him for all the intentional details
He puts into the thoughtful and caring
ways He loves you.

Her Purpose

Psalm 138:8

Dear Lord,

I pray my future wife would realize Your purpose for her life. I pray Your purposes would be her whole heart's desire. I pray You would reveal to her Your amazing plan for her life and our future marriage. Lord, give me the eyes to see what You have for her and how I can lead her toward that purpose. I pray Your plan for our marriage would be fulfilled in us, and that we would dedicate our lives together by submitting to Your will for us. Lord, if she ever loses sight of Your purpose for her life, I pray You would use me to gently guide her back to it. Give me the strength to stand with her and for her when she can't stand on her own. Please bring mature Christian women into her life that will constantly pour into her Your truth and perspective. May these women help her to see her amazing potential and the power You have given her to fulfill Your will. Use them to show her how You will use her in our marriage and in this world for Your glory. I pray she would see in herself what You see in her. I pray she would fully give her life over to You and trust what You are going to use her for. Make her so secure in You that she never questions You or doubts what You are doing, but always trusts You and follows You. Show me how I can continue to pray for her purpose and direction as I wait for her to be my bride.

In Jesus' name AMEN!

Confidence In You

Jeremiah 17:7

Dear Lord,

If this world and our enemy is constantly trying to make me question my relationship with You, and trying to make me doubt who You are and who I am in You, then I know that they are doing the same to my future wife. I pray You would give her a supernatural confidence in You, Lord! Show her who You are daily by the blessings You pour into her life, by the healing You bring to her mind, body and spirit, and by Your presence being ever present in her life. May those closest to her love her like she has never been loved before. I pray my future wife would find security in You. I pray she would praise You for being her everything. I pray her trust in You would not waiver, but would grow stronger every day. I pray she would run to You with every hurt and every joy. Increase her faith! May she find shelter in Your love and strength in Your joy. Pour so much grace into her life that it is impossible for her to forget who You are and who she is in You. Make her confidence contagious. I pray other women would admire her because of You. Use her to attract others to You. Use her right now to encourage other women in their faith. Use her to bring others to a place of security like she has with You. If anyone is trying to confuse her or distract her from her confidence in You, please remove those people far from her life. Cut them off today. Fortify her faith and strengthen her resolve to follow You with everything.

In Jesus' name AMEN!

Patien
Wa

Hey, Keep Waiting!

There are a few ways you can love your future bride today: patiently waiting for her, praying for her, saving yourself for her, and seeking God with all your heart, mind, soul, and strength, so that you become the man God wants you to be for her.

Wisdom With Finances

Hebrews 13:5

Dear Lord,

I pray for my future wife to have a healthy perspective of money. I pray she would not be in massive debt and if she is, I pray You would guide her to work diligently to get out of debt as soon as she possibly can. I pray she would be content. Let her trust in You for her finances, and keep her far from the love of money. I pray she would understand that having money is not wrong, but to be aware that how she treats money and how she uses money is important to You. You care that she is wise with how she manages the money You have given to her and entrusted to her. Lord, I also pray my future wife would be a generous person with her time and money. I pray she would be someone that is not stingy with others, but is abundantly open handed with the resources You have blessed her with. I pray people would look up to her for wisdom in this area of finances. Teach my future wife how to serve You alone, especially with her finances. I pray she is never enticed or tempted to spend more than what she has to spend. I pray she is never a slave to debt, but that her only outstanding debt is the debt of loving others. You caution in Your Word to be aware that the desires of wealth are deceitful and can choke out our effectiveness for You, so I pray she will not be deceived into chasing after wealth and things of this world, but would fervently seek wholeheartedly after You.

In Jesus' name AMEN!

Making Wise Decisions

Proverbs 12:15

Dear Lord,

Thank You for my future wife. I lift her up to You today and ask that she would be growing into a wise woman. May she seek after You and pursue godly wisdom by reading Your Word and praying daily. I pray she is surrounded by wise counsel. Surround her with seasoned and wise people who will help guide and lead her in Your ways. I pray her heart is humble and always willing to learn. If there are any foolish tendencies in her, please remove them, and mold her into a mature woman. I pray my future wife fears You and has a deep reverence for You. When she is making decisions I pray she would submit herself and her plans to You. Speak to her heart. Direct her steps. When she hears people teach about You, I pray she would test everything according to Your Word, determined to always seek after Your truth. Help her not to go astray. I pray she would love the pursuit of wisdom and that she would be passionate about learning and growing. I pray she would invest in her education whether through research, schooling, reading, or any other pursuit of knowledge that You desire of her. Help her to let go of pride and the desire to always be right in her own eyes. Help her to listen intently. Mold her into a woman of understanding. I pray her experiences now will contribute to the wisdom she will have as a wife in the future.

In Jesus' name AMEN!

Challenge

- #3 -

WRITE
God a letter

Share with Him your whole heart.

Include your hopes and fears for marriage, and
what you are currently feeling or experiencing.

Her Health

1 Corinthians 6:19—20

Dear God,

You have given my future wife a body that You desire for her to take care of and protect. I pray she would understand what Your Word says about her body being a temple of Your Holy Spirit. I pray she would strive to take care of her body as a way of worshipping You. I pray she would take her health seriously. If she has any bad habits, please help her replace them with good ones. Help her everyday to make good choices for her health. I pray she would consider what she eats, what she drinks, how she exercises, and how these things maintain the gift of a body You have given to her. May she also have balance in all of these things. May she be active, full of energy, and full of life. If there is anyone in her life who is encouraging unhealthy behavior and an unhealthy attitude toward her health, I pray You would either convict those people and change them to be good influences, or remove them from her life altogether. Surround my future bride with many friends and family members who care about her health as much as You do. People who will cheer her on and keep her accountable to Your desire for her to be a healthy and active part of Your body. Lord, if there is any history of disease or illness in her family, anything that may have been passed down through her DNA that could harm her or her future, I pray You would eradicate it right now! Protect her from it and make her body whole.

In Jesus' name AMEN!

Integrity

Proverbs 10:9

Dear Lord,

Thank You for my future wife. Thank You for creating her, and thank You for loving her. I pray she is a woman who walks in integrity. I pray she strives to live a righteous life. I pray she is a honest woman motivated to live according to Your truth. I pray she makes good decisions. I pray that any choices she is confronted with, would be carefully evaluated by her with caution and concern. Help her not to be hasty or selfish in the things she decides to pursue. Lead her, Lord! I pray her yes is her yes and her no is no. Help her to understand what priorities she should be focusing on. Help her not to be distracted from them. I pray she never quits a job without finishing it. I pray she never quits on people. May she be a woman of her word and stick to the agreements she makes. I pray she never steals or takes advantage of others. I pray she never cheats either. I pray she feels deep conviction about lying, even if they are small lies. I pray against sin in her life. Help her to be above reproach. Help her to take the honest and righteous path, even if it is more difficult. If there are situations from her past where she has sinned by stealing, cheating, or lying, please urge her to repent and reconcile. I pray You would prepare her for our future marriage by transforming her heart and her character, making her a wife of integrity.

In Jesus' name AMEN!

Resisting The Enemy

James 4:7

Dear God,

Thank You for my future wife, who You are preparing for me. The enemy would like nothing more than to stop us from having a powerful marriage, let alone a healthy marriage. I pray my future wife would learn how to see the tactics of the enemy and resist him. I pray she would fight to protect her purity. I pray she would fight to protect her faith. I pray she would fight against her flesh and walk in the Spirit. Father, teach my future wife to recognize temptation for what it is. Remind her that You always give her a way out. Help her to make the right choice to avoid sin and temptation. I pray she never puts herself in a position that would cause her to stumble and fall, or be taken advantage of. Remind her that You have given her freedom and victory in Christ, that she no longer has to give into temptations. I pray she would have a deep understanding of what it means to be free in Christ, that she is no longer slave to sin, that she has been given every provision to resist the devil, and resist the desires of the flesh. Holy Spirit, I ask that You would strengthen her and protect her from the enemy. I pray my future wife would listen to You far above ever listening to the deceit of the enemy. When she feels weak, be her strength. When she feels tempted, help her to run from that temptation. Teach her how to repent of her sin and live a life of righteousness.

In Jesus' name AMEN!

Broth
Chr

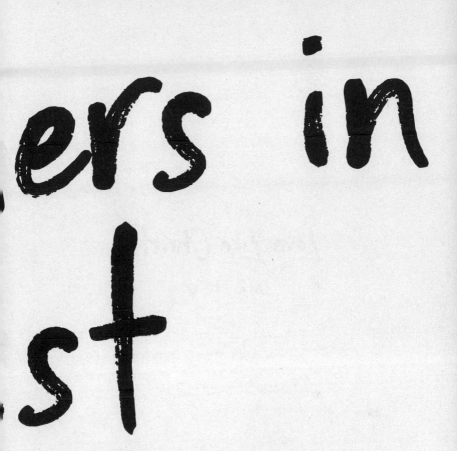

ers in
st

Spending time in fellowship with other believers and with God will protect your heart from the sting of loneliness, and it will mature you as a Christian man.

Love Like Christ

John 15:12-13

Dear Heavenly Father,

Thank You for the example of love Christ courageously lived out. I pray my future wife spends time meditating on Your love, soaking it up, and praying for her heart to love just as boldly. I pray she has many other examples in her life of Christ's love through the people who are around her. I pray her parents would show her what it looks like to love You and love each other well. I pray mentors would guide her to a place she understands Your love better and the power Your love has to transform her life and the lives of others. I pray my future bride would have an extraordinary love for others. I pray her life would be an example of Your love, and that she would teach others how to love through the things she does that are motivated by Your love in her. May she be kind, compassionate, caring, and generous. May she always be willing to do Your will empowered by Your love. I pray she is brave, and that she never lets fear keep her from loving others. I pray You would use her to reach people in this world who feel unloved. May Your Holy Spirit anoint her and fill her heart with love that overflows into the lives of others every day. I also pray that she has a great love for me. I pray our marriage reflects You because of how we love each other.

In Jesus' name AMEN!

Abundant Gentleness

1 Corinthians 4:1

Dear Lord,

I lift up my future wife to You and ask that You would bless her. Comfort her heart, and remind her that You are near. I pray she is a woman who pursues her relationship with You every day of her life. I pray she desires that her character reflects Your character. I pray the fruits of the Spirit are evident and abundant in her life. I pray her heart is soft and that her touch is gentle. I pray my future wife is humble and patient in every situation she finds herself in. I pray she is willing to bear with others in love. I pray she is a peacemaker. I pray she makes every effort to keep peace in all of her relationships. I pray for abundant gentleness to be a quality that others identify in her and appreciate her for. I pray she is gentle with her words, gentle in her actions, gentle with children, and gentle toward her parents. I pray she is meek and desires Your joy to fuel her. Please prepare her heart for our future marriage. I pray she is gentle toward me, and that she desires to be a peacemaker in our relationship. When conflict arises, please help her to face it with wisdom leading her heart and her thoughts. I pray she is merciful and full of grace. Holy Spirit, please be the gentleness in her life that helps her understand how to express gentleness toward others. Give her the gift of a tender heart.

In Jesus' name AMEN!

Challenge

— #4 —

WRITE
another letter

This time a response to your letter to God,
from God's perspective.

What do you think He would say
to encourage you?

Good Friends

Proverbs 13:20

Dear God,

Thank You for the gift of friendship. I pray my future wife has really strong Christian friendships in her life. I pray these friendships encourage her and affirm her. May these friends in her life be used by You to mature her and teach her why community is significant. I pray the company she keeps around her influences her more toward You. I pray the friends she has are wise and make healthy and righteous choices. I pray these friends and my future wife encourage each other to be world changers and to pursue Your purposes. I pray these friends would be supportive of my future wife, and that they would be a source of joy in her life. I also pray that my future wife has friends who are strong Christian wives. I pray she receives a positive perspective about marriage from them. I pray she learns more about Your design of marriage from them. Use these friends to prepare her for our future marriage. I pray that all of these friends would be protective of my future wife, always looking out for her well-being. I pray they challenge her to grow and mature in You. I pray they challenge her to never give up, to persevere, to endure even through the most difficult of situations. I pray that they would pray for each other and always point each other back to You. I pray they would keep each other accountable to knowing You better. I pray she learns how to be a good friend so that when we do get married, we would be the best of friends!

In Jesus' name AMEN!

Fill Her With Peace

Philippians 4:4-7

Dear Lord,

I pray my future wife experiences abundant peace in her life. If there is anything in her life that is causing her to be anxious, fearful, or worried, I pray she would stop to pray to You and present her worries as requests to You. Help her heart to trust You more. I pray she would never let fear rule her heart. I pray anxious thoughts never consume her mind. May Your peace guard her always. May You overwhelm her soul with the security of Your presence. When storms come, may Your peace comfort her. When things do not make any sense to her, may Your peace calm her spirit. When she is confused, may Your peace help her discern the truth. When conflict arises, may Your peace bring resolution. Show her where she can find Your peace. I pray she understands how thankfulness can combat worry. Bring to the front of her mind all the things she can praise You for. Help her to thank You every day. May Your Word be brought to the surface of her heart and mind, reminding her that You are her help. When she is anxious or scared, I pray she goes straight to You in prayer. I pray that You would prepare my future wife for marriage by extinguishing her fears about intimacy, her worries about us connecting, or any other anxious thoughts she may have. Fill her with Your peace so that she lives confidently!

In Jesus' name AMEN!

Serving Others

1 Peter 4:10-11

Dear Heavenly Father,

You are awesome and worthy of praise! Thank You for the gift of life You have given. Thank You for Your amazing grace. I praise You for Your everlasting love. I lift up my future wife to You today and ask that You would speak to her heart. Encourage her through any trial she is currently facing. Draw her close to You. Remind her of her immense value, and affirm her in ways only You can. I know You equipped her with specific talents and gifts for the purpose of revealing Yourself to the world. I believe she is incredibly gifted. Please show her how to use every gift You have given to her, and show her how these gifts will benefit and bless others. I pray she would be eager to use every gift she has to honor You. I pray she would use her gifts to serve others joyfully. I pray she would use her gifts to serve her family. Cultivate new gifts in her, and reveal to her the significance of them. Let people share with her how much she has blessed them to reassure her to never bury her gifts. Let her know the blessing she is. I pray she would rely on You for strength, and that she would never grow weary of doing good. I pray my future wife would know that You are the giver of good gifts, and that Your grace is abundant. I pray that You are glorified in everything she does. May her heart to serve You bring You joy!

In Jesus' name AMEN!

Her Attitude

Philippians 2:14-16

Dear Lord,

I pray for my future wife and ask that You would give her a positive attitude. I know how attitude can influence the whole day. I pray her attitude would never get in the way of Your will for her life. I pray her attitude is a positive influence in the lives of others. I pray others would desire to be like her because her attitude is so appealing. I pray her attitude would be an indicator to others of the hope she has in You. I pray my future bride is a cheerful worker. No matter what job or situation she is in, please help her to do what she does with an indescribable and contagious joy. May Your Holy Spirit enable her to be strong, resisting complaint when obstacles present themselves. I pray she is not easily angered, and that she does not operate with a sense of entitlement. Help her to be a person of understanding and a person who is grateful. I pray her attitude reflects happiness. I pray her attitude is never determined by the circumstances she is in, but rather determined by her faith in You. Holy Spirit, please help her to never grumble or complain about the things she is called to do. I pray her smile is a reflection of her heart, and I pray she is a bright light in this dark world. Help her to never labor in vain or pursue selfish gain. May her attitude and her heart reveal her faith and trust in You.

In Jesus' name AMEN!

Purity =

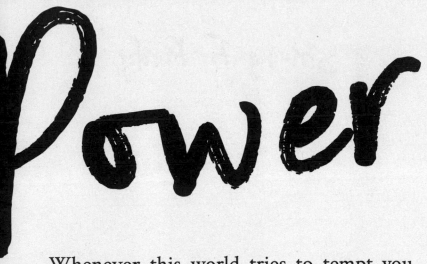

Power

Whenever this world tries to tempt you with the lust of the flesh, remember that purity is power, and God calls you to be pure as He is pure.

Striving For Purity

Hebrews 13:4

Dear Heavenly Father,

Thank You for today. Thank You for giving me perseverance and patience. Please help me to continue to pray for my future wife and our future marriage. I pray that hope in my heart grows abundantly for the future we will have together. I pray my future wife would be determined to live a life of purity. I pray that it is a priority to her. I pray she would understand the significance of purity, how it honors You, and how it will protect our future marriage. Give her wisdom in this area of her life. Help her to avoid situations where she can fall into temptation or be taken advantage of. I pray against any temptation in her life that would lead her to sin. I pray against the bondage of addiction, and I pray against the temptation of pornography. I pray against men with evil intentions. Protect the heart of my future wife, and protect her body. I pray she is a strong woman, who does not rely on the approval and affirmation of the world. I pray she would be pure in her thoughts, in her actions, and in her speech. May the purity in her life be a reflection of her commitment to You and love for You. I pray her purity would inspire other women to also strive for purity in their lives. I pray her purity is carried into our future marriage, and that my future wife would be an encouragement to me to also live a life of purity.

In Jesus' name AMEN!

Keep Her Safe

Psalm 28:7

31 Prayers For My Future Wife

Dear Lord,

I pray You would protect my future wife. Keep her life far from danger. This world is growing cold, and evil seems to be lurking everywhere. I pray You would keep her safe. Please give her an abundance of wisdom so that she never puts herself in a situation that leaves her vulnerable to attack. I pray she is determined to keep her mind sober so that she can think clearly. I also pray protection over her heart and her emotions. May she be strong and resist being pulled back and forth by those who try to manipulate her. Please keep anyone who seeks to harm her, far from her. I pray against the enemy and his schemes to tear her down or destroy her. I pray You would be her strength and her shield. Be her safe harbor in times of distress. May she find security in Your arms! I pray she trusts You and listens to You as You lead her. Preserve her life, Lord. Guard her mind from insecurities, from mean things that people say, and from any lies directed at her. Please care for my future bride. Provide for every need that she has. I pray she is smart to stay away from dangerous situations, and that she carries that same protective nature into our future marriage. Shield our marriage from the flaming arrows of the enemy! Develop in her an intuition to keep her life far from evil.

In Jesus' name AMEN!

Challenge
- #5 -

LET GOD
get to know you

Especially the parts that you are good at hiding.

If there is sin in your life, take a moment
to repent and be reconciled to God.

Victory In Christ

1 Corinthians 15:57

Dear Lord,

Thank You for loving my future wife. Thank You for protecting her and providing for her. I pray she acknowledges how much You cherish her. I also pray she understands the victory she has in Christ. I pray she can walk confidently in this life, knowing that You have set her free from the bondage of sin. I pray she receives forgiveness and grace for the mistakes she has made. I also pray that she forgives herself. Do not let shame oppress her. Do not let guilt overwhelm her. Set her free from the torture of embarrassment. I pray she rises above her mistakes, wholeheartedly repents, and walks with You in holiness. Please show her how she is holy through You. Give her a passion to pursue holiness and celebrate victory. Help her to fully understand that You are the only One who can help her escape the sting of death, the humiliation of mistakes, and heal her completely. Transform her heart, Lord! May she live with confidence and courage. May Your truth saturate her soul and satisfy her. I pray for healing in her life. I pray she never justifies her sin or goes back to it after repentance. I pray You would prepare her heart for marriage by granting her victory in her life. May she be an encourager to me to walk in victory every day we get to spend together. May we cheer each other on as we pursue oneness with each other and with You.

In Jesus' name AMEN!

A Heart Of Reverence

1 Samuel 12:24

Dear Heavenly Father,

I pray my future wife has a heart of reverence toward You. I pray she respects You and does everything to honor You. I pray she serves You faithfully with all of her heart. I pray she is aware of the great things You have done for her. May she praise You all the days of her life. I pray she submits herself to You in prayer and remains faithful to being obedient to Your ways. I pray my future bride fears You. I pray she submits her plans to You and trusts You leading her through them or rerouting her plans altogether. May her heart be yielded to You in every area of her life. I also pray that as a wife she has a heart of submission toward me. I pray she would fulfill her role that You designed for her to follow me as her head of authority. I also pray that You prepare my heart to lead her properly. I pray our future marriage is a reflection of Your love story. I pray my love for her and my leadership, reflects Christ and His love for His bride, the Church. I pray her submissive heart and respect for me reflects the love of the Church. I pray my future wife would feel like the most cherished wife in the whole world. I pray she would respect me, not only because You asked her to, but that she desires to because of the way I love her well. I pray Your will would be done.

In Jesus' name AMEN!

No Fear

John 14:27

Dear God,

I pray there is nothing in life that causes my future wife to be terrified. I pray she would not suffer from fear. Give her an understanding of who You are and the power that You have to help her through anything. I pray she confidently believes that You are with her. May she experience Your peace when moments tempt her to fear. I pray her heart is never troubled. I pray she never wrestles with worry or being afraid for any reason. Help her to control her emotions. I pray her emotions never cause her to respond out of the flesh. I pray she always operates and responds to situations with a sound mind. May family and friends be there for her during moments of panic or anxiety to reassure her and point her back to You. May the love and encouragement of others be a potent reminder of Your presence in her life. No matter what conflict or obstacle or trial she faces, I pray that she faces it all with faith. If there is ever a situation she endures that scares her, please immediately give her an increase of Your peace. I pray against stress and worry in her life. Release the pressure of this world off of her shoulders. Help her to relax, to breathe, to think clearly, and to act without sin. I pray she is a woman who is unwavering in her faith, able to stand strong in every circumstance.

In Jesus' name AMEN!

A Pr
Cr

found

ation

Marriage is one of the most profound and powerful things God ever created. It is not something to walk into lightly, and it should never be pursued without deep consideration.

Hunger For Knowledge

Proverbs 18:15

Dear Heavenly Father,

Thank You for my future wife. Thank You for her beautiful life. I trust that You are keeping her safe, and preparing her heart for mine. Thank You for inspiring me to pray for her. I love You, Lord! I pray specifically for her heart toward knowledge today. I pray she passionately seeks to learn as much as she can about everything. Give her a hunger for knowledge. Give her an insatiable desire to know more. I pray she appreciates learning and finds value in research. Whether she is pursuing an education through college, a technical school, a particular career, or venturing into entrepreneurship, I pray you would anoint her ability to process information, understand it, and retain it. I pray she would be quick to learn new skills. May her intelligence continue to grow as she acquires more knowledge. I pray she is also willing to learn skills necessary for being a wife and maintaining responsibilities in a home setting. Gift her the ability to fulfill her desires to serve our future marriage. Bless her with abilities that will help her fulfill the purposes You desire her to fulfill. Equip her with everything she needs to abide in Your will. I also pray that she has a hunger to invest as a wife into knowing everything she can about marriage. May she be willing to absorb and process information that will contribute to the strength and fortification of our future marriage.

In Jesus' name AMEN!

Fruits Of The Spirit

Galatians 5:22–23

Dear Lord,

I pray a blessing over my future wife. I pray for an abundance of fruit to be evident in her life. May her relationship with You be incredibly intimate. I pray she opens up to You and communicates to You what she is going through. I pray she is filled to the brim of her heart with satisfaction simply because she knows You. Holy Spirit, spend time with her, comforting her when she stumbles, and convicting her heart to repent. I pray her character continues to mature. May the fruits of Your Spirit grow wildly in her life because she gives You permission to transform her. I pray she is a woman who loves well, loves creatively, and loves selflessly. I pray joy is always radiating from her smile. I pray Your peace is so saturated in her life that others are impacted by it. May patience motivate her every response, and may her kindness leave others smiling. I pray my future wife is a good woman. I pray she is faithful in everything. Holy Spirit, show her how the fruit of gentleness can be a gift to those around her. I pray my future wife has self-control in every area of her life. Graph into her character Your good character, and cut-off any dead branches that are weighing her down and not producing fruit. Prepare her character for marriage. Equip her with virtue. Anoint her with rich soil so that exposure to Your Word continues to produce fruit in her life and fruit in our future marriage. May others taste Your goodness because of the fruit in her life.

In Jesus' name AMEN!

Maturing Her

1 Corinthians 14:20

Dear Lord,

You mold people's hearts like clay in the potter's hands. Thank You for being so intentional to form and transform something so beautiful. Thank You for my future wife. I pray You would mature her into the woman You created her to be. I pray she submits her life to You, and that she allows You to mold her, transform her, and mature her heart. May she be a woman who embraces responsibility. I pray she acts respectfully in all circumstances. I pray she carries herself with dignity and self-respect. May she be a woman who is modest and humble. May her choice of dress, behavior, and language reflect a heart that desires holiness. I pray You would cultivate a desire for intimacy in her heart. May she be courageous to share her whole heart with You and one day share it with me. I pray she would put childish ways behind her. I pray she is a refined woman, transformed by Your amazing grace. May she pursue wisdom and strive to live a holy life. Although I pray that my future wife is mature, I pray she also knows when to have fun and play around. Remove foolishness from her, and help her to understand how to behave appropriately during any given circumstance. Mature my future wife's character, her perspective, her attitude, and prepare her for all that You have for her.

In Jesus' name AMEN!

Saying No To Pride

Proverbs 11:2

Dear Heavenly Father,

I pray my future bride refuses to be prideful. I pray she would never boast about herself, but that she would boast about You. I pray she would have a humble heart. I pray against selfishness, and I pray against the temptation to fight for being right. I pray she fights for our future marriage and the sanctity of it. I pray she fights for peace. I pray she fights to protect our oneness. I pray she fights to keep us united at all cost. Please strip her heart of any pride, and replace it with a desire to be humble and gentle. Fill her with a passion to always lean back on Your Word to help her process her thoughts and her beliefs. I pray that pride never destroys our relationship. I pray we would be quick to dissolve conflicts that are being fueled by pride. Help us both to stop and pray for reconciliation. I pray we both have self-control and self-restraint. Help us to let go of issues that are not relevant, and help us to let You heal wounds that You are trying to mend. Bless my future wife. Mold her and shape her character to reflect Your character. Like diamonds that are found and polished, may Your Holy Spirit unearth her beauty and refine her. If she stumbles, please hold her up with Your righteous right hand. If she sins, may You forgive her and help her experience victory in her life. May You be glorified through her and through the testimony she has of knowing You and loving You with her whole heart.

In Jesus' name AMEN!

Challenge
- #6 -

SPEND TIME
in prayer

Spend 31 minutes praying only for your
future wife and your future marriage.

Preparing Her Heart

Ephesians 5:22–28

Dear Lord,

I pray You would prepare my future wife for our future marriage. I pray she would have a deep understanding of her role as a wife and what it means to be my helpmeet. Lord, I ask that she would be prepared for the uncertainties that may arise in our marriage or trials that we will face together. Give her endurance to stand faithfully by my side. I pray she would have a heart to follow me as I lead her. Give her a heart of submission and trust. I ask that she is willing to be vulnerable with me, sharing her whole heart with me. I pray she is willing to communicate transparently, without ever feeling like she needs to hide things from me. I pray she would never feel embarrassed or insecure around me. Prepare her heart for the permanence of our future marriage covenant. I pray against separation anxieties that might try to overwhelm her heart, making her feel an intense need to go back to her family. Help her transition when we move in together, and help her to feel comfortable. I pray she continues to seek You every day. Give her a profound understanding of what it means to be a wife and what oneness looks like in marriage. I pray You would prepare both of our hearts to serve one another with joy, to pursue peace, to love extravagantly, and to initiate intimacy.

In Jesus' name AMEN!

Intimacy With God

John 14:21

Dear Heavenly Father,

Thank You for the gift of intimacy. I pray my future wife passionately pursues an intimate relationship with You. I pray she is obedient to Your commands, and that she loves You with all of her heart. Reveal Yourself to her in mighty ways. Make Yourself known to her, and write Your Word on her heart. I pray she is willing to experience intimacy with You. I pray she lets You get to know who she really is. Holy Spirit, please speak softly to her, and guide her through life. Teach her Your ways, Lord. Show her how to live a holy life. I pray her heart always desires to draw closer to You! I pray my future wife abides in You. I pray she has a deep love for Christ and His mission. I pray she has an intense desire for Your will to be done in her and through her. I pray her faith is a solid foundation that is fortified when we get married. I pray we both understand that You are the most significant priority, even above our relationship. If my future wife needs healing for anything in her past, I pray that the intimacy You and her experience now would lead to that healing soon. I also pray that if I have any brokenness from my past and need healing, I would experience that soon. Prepare our hearts for one another by mending any brokenness or pain we have endured from our past. I pray our daily commitment to reading Your Word and praying would satisfy us and help us experience intimacy with You like we never have before.

In Jesus' name AMEN!

Our Future Wedding

Revelation 19:6-9

Dear God,

I pray for our future wedding. I pray that we would be able to work together to dream up and plan every detail of our special day. I pray against the enemy from any schemes to stop us from getting married or making the wedding day a disaster. I pray my future wife would have immense peace leading up to, and during, our future wedding. I pray our families would come together to support us and collaborate in harmony with us to celebrate our marriage. I pray against any conflict, any selfishness, and any tension that may arise because of our future wedding. If there is any issue that comes up, please be faithful to help us resolve it peaceably. I pray my future bride and I would be sober-minded about the day, focusing on giving You the glory for bringing us together, and putting more weight into what comes after the wedding. I pray You would prepare both of our hearts for our future marriage. I pray You would anoint our hearts with patience while we wait for our future wedding. Thank You for our future wedding with You. I pray my future wife and I are blessed to be invited to the wedding supper of the Lamb! Prepare us as Your bride for the return of Christ. I pray our perspectives are never skewed or driven by selfish ambition. Give us hearts that are focused on Your Kingdom and devoted to fulfilling Your perfect will. I pray others would come to know You through us. I pray those who attend our future wedding would be a witness of Your powerful truth, Your amazing grace, and Your extravagant love. I pray that through our future wedding, Your love story is revealed and that You are glorified!

In Jesus' name AMEN!

Unreal

Expec

istic

tations

Unrealistic expectations will get in the way of your oneness with your future bride. Ask God to help you to have a godly and Biblical perspective of the kinds of things you should expect from your marriage and bride.

Our Future Marriage

Ecclesiastes 4:9-12

Dear Lord,

Thank You for the gift of marriage. Thank You for designing and establishing marriage. Thank You for giving me a desire to get married, and thank You for revealing to me how marriage is a reflection of Your love story. I pray a blessing over my future wife. Please bless our future marriage. Use our marriage for Your glory. Continue to reveal to us what Your purposes are for our marriage. I pray our marriage is an encouragement to other married couples. Please help us find a strong community of Christian married couples who will walk through life with us, affirm us, and always point us back to You. I pray against pride. I pray we would seek to fulfill each other's needs above our own. Holy Spirit, transform our hearts and our perspectives to embrace oneness in marriage. I pray we would persevere when trials tempt us to give up. I pray we would leave a legacy of true love. Use my future wife and I to encourage each other, to lean on each other, to comfort each other, to cheer each other on toward Your will. I pray we would be each other's best friend from now until forever. May our love only increase as we celebrate every day we have together. I pray that the foundation of our future marriage would be established on Christ, our Rock and Redeemer! May You always remain at the center of our relationship.

In Jesus' name AMEN!

Our Future Oneness

Genesis 2:22-24

Dear God,

Thank You for the extraordinary gift of marriage. Thank You for listening to my desires, hopes, and prayers for our future marriage. I pray You would continue to prepare my heart for marriage and teach me what I need to know about being a husband. I pray for our future oneness in marriage. I pray You would show my future wife and I the significance of pursuing oneness in marriage. I pray we are always on the same page, and when our opinions do differ from each other, that we are quick to listen and seek understanding. Unite our hearts as one. I pray over our intimacy and ask that You would bless us. I pray You would help me as her husband to lead her according to Your Word. I pray we would recognize when we are getting in the way of being one with each other. Open our eyes to any selfish ways we have and transform us. Help us to fight for oneness. Give us courage and strength to walk in humility every day. May Your Holy Spirit motivate us to keep our relationship as a significant priority in our lives. I pray we would experience abundant unconditional love in our marriage. I pray we would passionately pursue peace every day. Lord, may Your will be done in us and through us as we pursue You and strive to fulfill Your will in our marriage.

In Jesus' name AMEN!

Challenge

- #7 -

WRITE
her a letter

Write a letter to your future wife.

Hold on to this until your wedding day,
then give it to her as a special gift.

Vows

My wife and I decided not to write our own vows when we got married. We went the traditional route and repeated the words our Pastor lead. Looking back at our wedding, and our relationship, there are some things we would have said if we did write our own vows. As we celebrate our 10th wedding anniversary January 6th, 2017, we decided to write out the words that we felt when we made our commitment to marriage, along with some words we have grown to understand deeper as we have experienced the richness of marriage over the last 10 years. We wanted to share these with you to inspire you to really consider the significance of your vows; whether you decide to make your commitment to marriage by using traditional vows, writing your own vows, or using these ones that we are sharing with you! Vows are a vital part of the wedding process, and the words you say on the altar are the foundation of your marriage covenant.

Vows To Her

I may never be able to give you the life you deserve.

I may never be able to give you the things your heart desires.

I may never be able to build you a dream home.

I may never have a bank account filled with money.

I know that there will be hard times and painful times.

I know there will be moments of doubt and fear.

There are many things that I will never be able to do for you, but the things that I can do I promise to do with all my heart.

I promise to love you even when you are unloveable and when I feel like I can't love anymore.

I promise to ask God to help me love you.

I promise to take care of you and our family to the best of my ability.

I promise to make you a priority over everything else in my life.

I promise to tell you anything and to let you tell me anything.

I will never stop pursuing my walk with God and my faith in His Son, Jesus Christ.

I will do everything I can to make Jesus the center of our marriage and home.

I promise to ask God daily to make our marriage into a powerful tool for His Kingdom. I will always have eyes for you and you alone.

I will always speak well of you to others, and I promise to encourage you. I promise to keep my heart pure for you.

I pray the Holy Spirit would keep me always growing closer to God and you.

I will protect our oneness at all cost.

I promise to keep my covenant with you always.

You are my gift and a promise fulfilled, and I will always be thankful and excited to have and to hold you.

I promise to steward your heart well in the strength God gives me every day.

Thank you for waiting for me.

Thank you for saying yes to God, and thank you for saying yes to me.

I love you.

Vows To Him

You are my best friend, forever.

I thank God for bringing you into my life.

You have shown me true love, and you have influenced my life for the better.

Thank you for choosing me to be yours alone.

Thank you for loving me like Christ.

Thank you for believing in my talents, and thank you for always pointing me toward God.

You are my biggest encourager, you are my greatest source of comfort besides God, and you are my favorite person in this world.

You are my answer to prayer.

I don't know what our future holds, but I do know God has big plans for us.

I know because we are both dreamers for His Kingdom and we desire to serve Him with everything we have.

I can't guarantee that we will never face hardship or unwanted trials, in fact, I am more positive that we will face challenges in this life, but as your wife, I promise to persevere together with you.

I promise to understand what it means to be one with you.

I promise to follow you and let you lead me and lead our family.

I promise to do my part to leave a legacy of love.

I promise to always point your heart toward God.

I promise to support your faith and encourage your love for the Lord.

I also promise to surrender my heart to God and pursue my own relationship with Him.

I promise to rely on Him to fulfill me and I commit to being obedient to His Word.

I promise to let Him change my heart so that I can be the wife He wants me to be for you.

I commit to learning and always investing into our marriage.

I promise to be respectful in my responses, and I promise to seek reconciliation with you at any sign of discord or tension.

I promise to cheer you on in life, to comfort you, to exhort you in your God-given desires. I promise to be faithful.

I promise to be loyal.
I promise to fight for our marriage.

I may never be perfect, but I promise to always strive for perfection and victory won through Christ alone.

I promise to hold your hand for as long as you want and grow old by your side, unless Jesus comes back before then.

I promise to love you through sickness, through doubt, through drought, and through financial depression.

I promise to stick closer than glue.

I commit my heart to finding security in God and not in the things of this world.

I commit to loving you despite our circumstances and whether or not our marriage is everything we ever hope for.

I promise to have fun with you and to laugh with you.

I promise to pray with you and pray for you.

I vow to intentionally pursue intimacy with you, and I commit my whole heart to loving you extravagantly.

I promise to give you my heart, to let you see the real me.

I promise to always be transparent with you, and I promise to share the deepest parts of me with you.

I promise to let you get to know me and I promise to spend time getting to know you, for the rest of our lives.

I promise to give you permission to speak truth into my life, to tell me when you see sin in my life, and I promise to purpose my heart to listen to you.

I promise to keep Christ at the center of our relationship, the foundation and cornerstone of our covenant.

A cord of three strands is not quickly broken.

You, me and Christ are intimately intertwined.

I promise, that even in our brokenness, I will hold on to what we have and never let it go.

I promise to make our marriage the most important priority in our life. I promise to pursue oneness with you.

I promise to pursue an extraordinary life with you.

I promise to do my part in our love story and love you well.

I promise to be your best friend, forever.

I love you and I always will, I promise.

Marriage After God

Getting married soon? Start your marriage off with a strong foundation and grab a copy of Marriage After God today!

marriageaftergod.com

Thirty-One Prayers For Your Spouse

Don't stop praying for your spouse after you get married make prayer a daily habit and a life long pursuit.

Husband & Wife After God 30-Day Devotionals

These two complementary marriage devotionals walk through important biblical marriage principles, while also addressing different areas of life that a husband and wife might struggle with. We wrote these devotionals to help husbands and wives grow closer to God and closer to each other.

Visit Our Online Book Store Today.
Shop.marriageaftergod.com

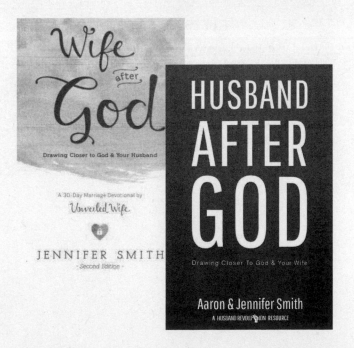

If this prayer book has impacted your faith please let me know by posting a testimony here:

31prayersformyfuturewife.com

For more marriage resources please visit:

shop.MarriageAfterGod.com

Sign-up for daily prayers by email:

husbandrevolution.com/daily-prayer/

Get connected:

Facebook.com/husbandrevolution
Instagram.com/husbandrevolution